MISSISSIPPIANS
ALL

Also by Frank E. Smith

MISSISSIPPIANS ALL

by Frank E. Smith and Audrey Warren

Pelican Publishing House

New Orleans   *1968*

PELICAN PUBLISHING HOUSE, New Orleans, La.
Manufactured in the United States of America by
KINGSPORT PRESS, INC., Kingsport, Tennessee

This book is dedicated to the many Mississippians, both black and white, who are working to improve the quality of life for all Mississippians.

Contents

Introduction by Frank L. Smith

The contributions of Mississippians to all phases of American life have been important throughout the more than 150 years that Mississippi has been a state. Over the years, many Mississippians have been acclaimed nationally and throughout the world for their achievements; and many more, who would have achieved national prominence if their work had been done in or near some of the big metropolitan centers, have been recognized for the superior quality of their work in many crafts and arts.

With the advent of increasingly better educational opportunities for all Mississippi citizens, we can look forward confidently to even greater contributions by Mississippians to American life, and at the same time to a steadily improving quality of life inside the state itself.

Valor and talent and enterprise are not exclusively Mississippi qualities, but pride in the achievements of those who belonged first to us is one of the essential ingredients of true community spirit. The achievements by Mississippians in recent years are well worth the attention and admiration of all of us today, and these brief sketches of the lives of eight Mississippians are presented so that we may all be mindful of what our own men and women have added to the heritage of the nation and of mankind.

For 150 years men from Mississippi have been prominent among the military heroes of our country. None, however, is entitled to greater glory than those special few who have been awarded the highest honor our country can bestow upon its citizens—the Medal of Honor. Sgt. Jake Lindsey and Pfc. Milton Olive are examples of the valorous Mississippi military men who have been awarded this great honor.

The quality of its creative and performing artists is an important measure of any civilization. Mississippi can be proud to have contributed to the world the outstanding American novelist of the twentieth century, William Faulkner. Our state can also take credit for two of the great women artists of our time—Eudora Welty and Leontyne Price. They exemplify the achievements of Mississippi women.

As examples of Mississippi political leaders and statesmen, it is fitting to present sketches of two who served as colleagues in the United States Senate, Blanche K. Bruce and Lucius Q. C. Lamar. Bruce is the foremost example of the ex-slaves freed by the Civil War who lifted themselves, largely by their own bootstraps, to great success and achievement after freedom. For nearly a quarter of a century he was recognized as the outstanding Negro political leader in the nation. His contributions to our state and nation are only beginning to be adequately assessed.

L. Q. C. Lamar was not only honored in Mississippi by election to the United States House of Representatives and Senate, but was accepted by political friend and foe alike as a leader among Southern Democrats during this same post-Civil War period. Belated national recognition of his great political courage in the best American tradition was given when Lamar was one of those sketched in John F. Kennedy's *Profiles in Courage.*

The achievements of Mississippi athletes in virtually every type of sport, both amateur and professional, have been recognized for many years. Track and field stars have become Olympic champions, and few states have as many natives active in the National and American Football Leagues. As representatives of Mississippi athletes, however, we have chosen two young men who fought their way to the top in the fiercely competitive world of major league baseball, Jake Gibbs and George Scott.

These brief sketches of eight Americans, Mississippians all, who have made an important contribution to their country, are presented in the hope that their records may instill pride in their fellow Mississippians and inspire the present generation of young Mississippians to strive toward similar accomplishments.

Technical Sergeant Jake W. Lindsey

Tec. Sgt. Jake W. Lindsey being presented to a joint session of the United States Congress, May 21, 1945. General of the Army George C. Marshall is reading his citation, and President Harry S. Truman is about to present the Medal of Honor.

Jake W. Lindsey

"For conspicuous gallantry and intrepidity at the risk of his own life, above and beyond the call of duty. . . ." So begins the roster of men whose combat heroism and sacrifice for their country and comrades were so extraordinary as to earn for them the highest military honor this nation can confer. They are few, the holders of the Congressional Medal of Honor. Among the more than twelve million soldiers, sailors and airmen who served in World War II, only 292 were awarded the Medal. One among those 292 was (and is) T/Sgt. Jake William Lindsey of Lucedale, Mississippi, a veteran of three assault landings and seven campaigns when his heroic, single-handed repulse of an enemy attack in Germany won him the award.

The battle for which he was cited (he had already received the Silver Star, the Purple Heart, and the Infantryman's Badge) lasted for four days and four nights in November 1944 in the Huertgen Forest in Germany. It occurred during a counterattack by the Germans. At the end of the third day, Sergeant Lindsey and six men were all that remained of his forty-man company. He had been wounded in the leg on the first day of battle.

On the fourth day he and his men took shelter in a large foxhole, still continuing to fight with one machine gun, two Browning automatic rifles and tommy guns.

Sgt. Lindsey was using a rifle with a tank grenade attachment. On that November 16, he recalled:

"I stopped the first tank when it was ten yards in front of me. Then the crew came out and we killed them. We knocked out a few hundred Germans [200 Germans were killed] and seven tanks before it was finished. At one point we were surrounded, and we called for our artillery to pour it on." The small group was finally relieved by another unit.

President Harry S. Truman bestowed the Medal of Honor upon Sgt. Lindsey at an unprecedented and cheering joint session of the Congress, the only time the Medal has been so awarded. Highest ranking officers of the military and naval commands and members of the Cabinet came and heard the tributes paid by the Commander-in-Chief to this 24-year-old, slight, wiry, and soft-speaking Mississippian, and through him, to all other American fighting men of great valor. The mother, father, and married sister of the sergeant were there also, sitting tense and proud. His brother James and his brother-in-law, Jack Smith, were with the Navy in the South Pacific.

The citation of the exploit which had won the sergeant the nation's highest distinguished combat award was read by General of the Army George C. Marshall, then Chief of Staff. As General Marshall read, the young man who had left high school in 1939 to enter the service stood beside him at rigid attention, apparently wanting it all to be over with quickly.

They stood awaiting the President while the assemblage cheered. Another ovation broke loose as the President, smiling broadly entered the chamber and walked at fast pace down the center aisle to the rostrum. Mounting it, he moved up to the sergeant, who broke attention only sufficiently to bow for the Medal to be slipped around his neck. Mr. Truman stepped around the sergeant and fastened the ribbon securely at the back. The sergeant gave a wide salute to the Commander-in-Chief, who extended his hand. Then he banged the sergeant on the back affectionately, and turned to address the Congress:

"We are assembled here today to confer the Nation's highest decoration on a young American soldier. It so happens that Technical Sergeant Jake W. Lindsey of Lucedale, Mississippi, is the one hundredth infantryman to receive the Medal of Honor in this war for bravery above and beyond the call to duty. Through him, we pay a grateful Nation's tribute to the courage of all our fighting men.

"The history of this war is filled with countless acts of valor by our soldiers and sailors and marines under fire. Those who win the Medal of Honor have displayed the highest quality of courage.

"We have heard in the citation what Sergeant Lindsey did. His inspiring deeds on the battlefield require no further praise from any man. They stand—with the deeds of the others on whom this decoration has been conferred—in the finest tradition of American heroism.

"This Medal, to repeat, is given for gallantry at the risk of life *beyond the call to duty*. No officer ordered Sergeant Lindsey to stand alone against a company of the enemy. No officer ordered him when wounded to engage eight Germans in hand-to-hand combat. Those decisions came from his own heart. They were a flash of the nobility which we like to think is a part of every American. They were the unselfish valor which can triumph over terrible odds. They were the very essence of victory.

*   *   *   *   *

"It seems fitting that in this symbolic ceremony we should honor an infantryman. There is little glamor in his service. He faces not only the enemy before him, but the cold and the heat, the rain and the snow, the dust and the mud, which so often makes his life miserable. These things he endures, and rises above them to such deeds as those we celebrate today.

"This is a proud and moving occasion for every American. It follows the complete victory of our Allied Forces over a powerful enemy in Europe. It finds us striking devastating blows in the Pacific. We are preparing to strike them later in overwhelming force.

"Before the battle against Japan is won, we shall have other men to honor—men whose deeds, like those we celebrate today, will have brought closer our inevitable victory.

"I hope that every man and woman in our Nation today will reverently thank God that we have produced such sons as these. With their high courage as an inspiration, we cannot fail in the task we have set for ourselves.

"It is with gratitude and pride that as President of the United States, and in the name of the Congress, I have presented this Medal of Honor to Technical Sergeant Jake W. Lindsey."

When the President, Cabinet members and others left and the Senate had filed back to its own smaller chamber, Sergeant Lindsey was taken downstairs to a Mississippi fish luncheon given by Representative William M. Colmer of his district. Mr. and Mrs. Lindsey and the sergeant's sister, Pauline, attended, along with the whole Mississippi Congressional delegation. The President looked in for a moment, then hurried back to this appointments at the White House.

More than half the men who have received the Medal of Honor in this century gave their lives in the heroic acts for which the Medal was awarded them. Sgt. Lindsey is one of the lucky ones. Mississippi has continued to be his home, and he has continued to serve with distinction in the United States Army.

General Orders
No. 43   Washington, D. C., 30 May 1945

Award of the Medal of Honor

By direction of the President, under the Joint Resolution of Congress approved 12 July 1862 (amended by act of 3 March 1863, and act of 9 July 1918), the Medal of Honor for gallantry and intrepidity at the risk of his life above and beyond the call of duty is awarded by the Department of the Army in the name of the Congress to:

Technical Sgt. Jake W. Lindsey, Sixteenth Infantry, who led a platoon reduced to 6 of its original strength of 40 in the attack on an enemy position near Hamich, Germany, on the 16th of November, 1944.

His men had captured their objective and were digging in when counterattacked by a German infantry company and five tanks. Armed with a rifle and grenades, Sergeant Lindsey took position on the left and in advance of the remainder of his platoon and although exposed to heavy rifle, machine gun, and tank fire beat off repeated enemy attacks. Tanks moved to within 50 yards of him but were forced to withdraw because of his accurate rifle and grenade fire.

After driving off the tanks he knocked out two machine guns to his front. Although painfully wounded, he continued firing and throwing grenades until his ammunition was expended.

An enemy squad attempted to set up a machine gun 50 yards from him. Unmindful of his wounds and enemy fire he rushed these 8 German soldiers, single-handedly closed with them, killed 3 with his bayonet and captured 3. Two others escaped.

In his fearlessness, inspiring courage, and superb leadership, Sergeant Lindsey carried on a brilliant defense of his platoon's hard-won ground, securing the position and inflicting heavy casualties on the numerically superior enemy.

Private First Class Milton Olive

Pfc. Milton Olive in jump uniform.

Milton Olive

Pfc. Milton Lee Olive III had not yet been born when Sgt. Lindsey stood embattled in that German forest, but twenty-one years later he was to join the long line of Mississippians who have earned the Medal of Honor. The war in which Milton Olive fought was half a world removed from Germany. The place in which he died was a jungle in Vietnam. A boy from Holmes County unhesitatingly gave his life so that his comrades in arms might live.

Milton Olive was born on a farm near Ebenezer, a village in Holmes County. His father was the son of Mr. and Mrs. Milton B. Olive, Sr. Mr. Olive, Sr., was a well known farmer in southern Holmes County, and Mrs. Olive taught school for a number of years at Durant. Milton's mother, whose maiden name was Clara Lee, was a native of Indianola. Milton Olive, Jr., moved to Chicago to seek employment, but Milton III was raised by his grandparents in Mississippi. After attending the Ebenezer grammar school, he moved on to the Saints High School in Lexington. His schoolmates remember him as a quiet, religious boy.

After enlisting in the Army at the age of seventeen, Private Olive volunteered for airborne infantry training, and received special courses at Ft. Sill, Oklahoma, and Ft. Knox, Kentucky. The young airborne trooper became a member of one of the Army's elite units, and he found that about one-fourth of its members were Negroes. He learned that Negro participation in American wars is as old as American history.

Negroes were members of the colonial groups who fought Indians in the years before the Revolution, and they then fought the English in the Revolutionary War. A Negro unit of 3,000 men won the particular praise of Commodore Oliver Hazard Perry in the War of 1812. Perry, the most famous American hero of that war, described his black troops as "insensible to danger," and praised them unstintingly.

In the Civil War more than 200,000 black men were recruited into the Union Army, and even the Confederacy began organizing Negro units toward the end of the war. Negro cavalrymen were among those killed with Custer at Little Big Horn, and it was a Negro unit which captured Geronimo and protected the Southwest from the ravages of Billy the Kid and his outlaws.

Some 10,000 Negroes enlisted for the Spanish-American War, and a black cavalry unit distinguished itself in support of Theodore Roosevelt's Rough Riders at the battle of El Caney.

Negro soldiers were still segregated in World War I, but the first experiments with integrated units began in the final months of combat in World War II. Segregation was officially ended during the Korean War.

Young Olive came home for a visit with his grandparents at Christmas 1964, and in the following July was shipped to Vietnam as a member of the 173d Airborne Brigade. To keep his grandparents back in Mississippi from worrying, Milton did not tell them about going overseas. They learned of his death only when his father made a special trip down from Chicago to tell them.

On October 22, 1965, just 16 days before his 19th birthday, Milton went out with his platoon on a search and destroy patrol in Viet Cong territory. With four other men he was moving along a jungle trail when an enemy grenade was thrown into their midst.

Shouting "Look out" to his comrades, Pfc. Olive instantly fell on the grenade, pulled it to his body, and took the full impact of the blast. At the ceremony in which he awarded the Medal of Honor post-humously to Milton Olive, President Lyndon B. Johnson said:

"There are occasions on which we take great pride, but little pleasure. This is one such occasion. Words can never enlarge upon acts of heroism and duty, but this nation will never forget Milton Lee Olive 3d.

"President Harry Truman once said that he would far rather have one Medal of Honor than to have been the President of the United States. I know what he meant. Those who have earned this decoration are very few in number. But true courage is very rare. This honor we reserve for the most courageous of all of our sons.

"The Medal of Honor is awarded for acts of heroism above and beyond the call of duty. It is bestowed for courage demonstrated not in blindly overlooking danger, but in meeting it with eyes clearly open.

"That is what Private Olive did. When the enemy's grenade landed on that jungle trail, it was not merely duty which drove this young man to throw himself upon it, sacrificing his own life that his comrades might continue to live. He was compelled by something that is more than duty, by something greater than a blind reaction to forces that are beyond his control.

"He was compelled, instead, by an instinct of loyalty which the brave always carry into conflict. In that incredible brief moment of decision in which he decided to die, he put others first and himself last. I have always believed that to be the hardest but the highest decision that any man is ever called upon to make.

"In dying, Private Milton Olive taught those of us who remain how we ought to live.

❂   ❂   ❂   ❂   ❂

"Men like Milton Olive die for honor. Nations that are without honor die, too, but without purpose and without cause. It must never be said that when the freedom and the independence of a new and a struggling people were at stake that this mighty, powerful nation of which we are so proud to be citizens would ever turn aside because we had the harassments that always go with conflict and because some thought the outcome was uncertain or the course too steep, or the cost too high.

"In all of this there is irony, as there is when any young man dies. Who can say what words Private Olive might have chosen to explain what he did? Jimmy Stanford and John Foster, two of the men whose lives he saved that day on that lonely trail in that hostile jungle 10,000 miles from here, are standing on the White House steps today because this man chose to die. I doubt that even they knew what was in his mind as he jumped and fell across that grenade.

"But I think I do know this: on the sacrifices of men

who died for their country and their comrades our freedom has been built. Whatever it is that we call civilization rests upon the merciless and seemingly irrational fact of history that some have died for others to live, and every one of us who enjoys freedom at this moment should be a witness to that fact.

"So Milton Olive died in the service of a country that he loved and he died that the men who fought at his side might continue to live. For that sacrifice his nation honors him today with its highest possible award."

Pfc. Olive was the third United States serviceman to be awarded the Medal of Honor for heroism in Vietnam. He was the first Negro to receive it in that conflict and the eighth of his race to be so honored in United States history.

Milton Olive is buried at the West Grove Missionary Baptist Cemetery near Lexington, eternal testimony to the knowledge that valor knows no nation, courage no geography, and loyalty no race.

General Order No. 18, dated April 26, 1966, at Washington, D. C., reads:

Award of the Medal of Honor

By direction of the President, under the Joint Resolution of Congress approved 12 July 1862 (amended by act of 3 March 1863, act of 9 July 1918 and act of 25 July 1963), the Medal of Honor for conspicuous gallantry and intrepidity at the risk of life above and beyond the call of duty is awarded posthumously by the Department of the Army in the name of the Congress to:

Private First Class Milton L. Olive, III, RA16810165, United States Army, who distinguished himself by conspicuous gallantry and intrepidity at the risk of his own life above and beyond the call of duty while participating in a search and destroy operation in the vicinity of Phu Cuong, Republic of Vietnam, on 22 October 1965. Private Olive was a member of the 3d Platoon of Company B, 2d Battalion (Airborne), 503d Infantry, as it moved through the jungle to find the Viet Cong operating in the area. Although the Platoon was subjected to a heavy volume of enemy gunfire and pinned down temporarily, it retaliated by assaulting the Viet Cong positions, causing the enemy to flee. As the Platoon pursued the insurgents, Private Olive and four other soldiers were moving through the jungle together when a grenade was thrown into their midst. Private Olive saw the grenade, and then saved the lives of his fellow soldiers at the sacrifice of his own by grabbing the grenade in his hand and falling on it to absorb the blast with his body. Through his bravery, unhesitating actions, and complete disregard for his own safety, he prevented additional loss of life or injury to the members of his platoon.

Private Olive's conspicuous gallantry, extraordinary heroism, and intrepidity at the risk of his own life above and beyond the call of duty are in the highest traditions of the United States Army and reflect great credit upon himself and the Armed Forces of his country.

Eudora Welty

Photo by Kay Bell

Eudora Welty in an informal moment.

Eudora Welty

Few states have contributed as many outstanding writers to modern American literature as has Mississippi. The famous names include such diverse and perceptive talents as Stark Young, author of *So Red the Rose*, and Richard Wright, author of *Native Son* and *Black Boy*. By far the best known is William Faulkner, perhaps the greatest American novelist of the twentieth century.

As in other artistic fields, Mississippi's contribution has not been limited to talented men. Active women writers include such widely recognized authors as Elizabeth Spencer, Ellen Douglas, Margaret Walker, and Berry Morgan. Among women writers today, however, Eudora Welty of Jackson is considered by most critics to be the best in the United States. For thirty years Miss Welty's fiction had delighted, and sometimes puzzled, a steadily growing audience no longer limited to American readers. She has, like Faulkner, immortalized a part of the Mississippi countryside that has moved into American literature as Eudora Welty's Mississippi.

Eudora Alice Welty was born at Jackson in 1909. Her parents, Christian and Mary Chestina Andrews Welty, were natives of Ohio and West Virginia who had moved to Jackson soon after their marriage. Mr. Welty became president of one of Mississippi's best known financial institutions, the Lamar Life Insurance Company, named for Senator L. Q. C. Lamar. Eudora was an only daughter who grew up with two brothers.

The Welty daughter was fortunate to grow up in a home where her precocious talents were encouraged by her parents. She became an avid reader while still a child, and the endless reading quickened, rather than dulled, a vivid imagination which drew the world and its past in bright and contrasting colors. While attending Central High School in Jackson, Eudora began to develop her writing ability in school activities, and she took lessons in painting after school. From Central High she went on to Mississippi State College for Women at Columbus. Coming in contact here with other talents and teachers, Eudora realized she could profit from an enlarged curriculum at a school better equipped for the training of a prospective writer. After two years at Columbus, Eudora transferred to the University of Wisconsin.

At Wisconsin she enrolled as an English major, and began a systematic study of some of the same writers she had been reading for many years. In addition, she received a formal introduction to the work of the great Russian novelists, and modern writers like Yeats, Virginia Woolf and William Faulkner.

Miss Welty received her bachelor of arts degree in English Literature at Wisconsin in 1929, but the degree carried no assurance of making a living, unless she became a teacher of English literature. Her father suggested that the next thing to writing for a living would be writing advertising, and so she was enrolled for a year in the Columbia University School of Business, with courses in writing and selling advertising. The most important part of this course, however, was exposure to the theater, concerts, and cultural opportunities of New York City. Miss Welty might have liked to stay near them, but after the year of schooling there were no jobs available in New York City in the first year of the great depression. She had to return to Mississippi to find work.

Jobs in Mississippi were scarce also, but her family's prominence helped her find part-time work related to her chosen field of writing. The Lamar Life Insurance Company owned Jackson's pioneer radio station, WJDX, and for a while Eudora was a part-time script girl, advertising writer, and performer of odd jobs that included cleaning the canary bird cage. For several years she wrote a weekly column about Jackson and Mississippi social events for the Sunday society section of the *Memphis Commercial Appeal.*

Like hundreds of other writers throughout the country, she had her first full-time job as a writer with the WPA (Works Progress Administration). Miss Welty was hired as a "Junior Publicity Agent" in 1933 and continued in this role until 1936. It was a period in which she really came to know Mississippi, especially the small towns and villages that were to provide the locale for so much of her future work. She traveled over the state, interviewing all types of people and watching all sorts of activities as she helped report the story of WPA in Mississippi at a time when the agency was the chief economic refuge of an area badly battered by the depression. Her job was to provide publicity for various WPA projects, and she did an exceptional job as a newspaperwoman for both the city dailies and the country week-lies. Hers was undoubtedly the most active and varied career for a newspaperwoman in the state up until that time.

Miss Welty not only wrote WPA publicity for the country weeklies; she read the papers avidly. In the columns of county correspondents she learned myriad details of rural and small town life. She built a large collection of Mississippiana. One of her prize items was a scrapbook of clippings of newspaper columns by country correspondents which preserved the real flavor of rural Mississippi. Much of her fiction has been about the same sort of people who wrote the columns, or were written about in them.

To provide good newspaper coverage for the WPA projects, she also had to provide pictures, so she had to learn how to take them. Characteristically, she became an expert photographer with the second-hand camera made available by the WPA. She also began to make special photographs of the small towns and rural coun-tryside, with unposed character studies of representative Negro citizens.

The Lugene Gallery, a camera and photography store in New York City, presented a month long exhibit of Miss Welty's photographic studies in 1936. The photo-graphs attracted a great deal of favorable comment, but no buyers from the publications just then beginning to specialize in photography. During this period Miss Welty had temporary hopes that photography might offer a method of entering the world of commercial jour-nalism, but the hopes faded after the one-man show produced no concrete offers for the use of her work.

The year 1936 was an important one in Miss Welty's career. State political conflicts caused her to lose her job with the WPA. She then went to work for the Mississippi Advertising Commission, a state agency established by Governor Hugh White to encourage tourists to visit the state and new industries to come in.

But by far the most important event of 1936 was the publication of her first short story, "Death of a Traveling Salesman," in the magazine *Manuscript*. *Manuscript* was a "little" magazine, an example of a literary phenomenon especially popular in the 1920's and 1930's. *Manuscript* was one of the most highly regarded of these magazines, and acceptance was a much-needed boost for the morale of an unpublished author. Miss Welty had been writing short stories from the time she returned to Mississippi after her sojourn in New York. This first acceptance, instead of a rejection, of her fiction was a major milestone.

Shortly afterwards she had a story published in *River*, a "little" magazine published at Oxford, Mississippi. *River* was one of the few of these ever published in Mississippi, and it survived only a few months, but the fact that it gave Eudora Welty her first recognition in Mississippi is now its chief claim to fame.

During this period Louisiana State University began publishing *The Southern Review*, a literary quarterly which won immediate acclaim throughout the country for its outstanding quality. During its first years Eudora Welty was the most promising Southerner published in the quarterly. The publication of her work has become part of the legend of *The Southern Review* when it was edited by Robert Penn Warren and Albert Erskine.

Some of these stories were included in the collection of short stories *A Curtain of Green*, published in 1941, which established her as one of the most noteworthy new writers. Katherine Anne Porter wrote an introduction to the book with lavish praise. There were enthusiastic reviews in major Eastern publications, but the enthusiasm was also evident in Mississippi. In the *Mississippi Literary Review* for November 1941, Dale Mullen published a critical essay (perhaps the first of hundreds that have since been published) on Miss Welty's work, including these comments:

"The point I wish to make is that she is a Mississippian and has felt Mississippi all about her. It has been easy in the last few years to become interested in Mississippi: there is a growing body of Mississippi literature; there have been many studies made and books written about the South, and there have been studies made and books written about Mississippi itself. Thus when she began to write, she wrote about that Mississippi which has fascinated such diverse writers as Faulkner, Cohn, Kroll, and Evans Wall.

"There is a thesis or an essay to be written on the idea that Mississippi writers are creating not simply a number of books but rather a body of literature. . . . Eudora Welty has undoubtedly been influenced by Mississippi's literature; her work has now become a part of it and is influencing and will influence more and more the work of all the state's writers.

"But do not imagine for a moment that Miss Welty's work is not superior to most Mississippi writing. In fiction only Faulkner has done better work."

With the impressive recognition which followed the publication of *A Curtain of Green,* Miss Welty was able to devote her full time to serious writing. Her first novel, *The Robber Bridegroom,* with a locale along the Natchez Trace, was published in 1942, followed by another collection of stories, *The Wide Net,* in 1943. The novel, *Delta Wedding,* came in 1946, and another collection of stories, titled *The Golden Apples,* in 1949. *The Ponder Heart* was a brilliantly comical long story or short novel first published in a single issue of the *New Yorker* in 1954, and later adapted into a highly successful Broadway play. She has published little since her last collection of short stories, *The Bride of Innisfallen,* in 1955. Her international audience has therefore been pleased to see the publication of individual short stories by Miss Welty in the last few years.

Many awards have come to her since the O. Henry Memorial Contest first-prize in 1942. Chief of them are the William Dean Howells Medal for "the most distinguished work of American fiction" for the period 1950–55 for *The Ponder Heart,* and election to the National Institute of Arts and Letters. A most significant recognition is the fact that her work appears in more anthologies than any other living American writer. Her books have been published in translations throughout Europe.

Miss Welty does not have an aggressive personality, but she has developed into a compelling and forceful teacher and lecturer on the art of writing fiction. Her essay *Place in Fiction* is a landmark of writing in this field. In this work she develops fully her thesis that great fiction depends upon the inevitability of the characters being placed exactly where they are because of the accumulated feelings which are associated with places. "Perhaps it is the sense of place that gives us the belief that passionate things, in some essence, endure," she has said. "Whatever is significant and whatever is tragic in a place live as long as the place does, though they are unseen, and the new life will be built upon those things—regardless of commerce and the way of rivers and roads and other vagaries."

Miss Welty can instruct from the platform, but she also entertains. Anyone who has heard her read one of her great short stories, *I Live at the P.O.*, will agree.

Eudora Welty is a Mississippian whose talent is helping to enrich the literary tradition of the whole world.

Leontyne Price

Photo courtesy RCA Victor

Leontyne Price in an informal moment.

Leontyne Price

Throughout history, the world has closely associated music with its events involving ceremony and pageantry. Musical events themselves have often become well known for glitter and pomp, as we know from the role of opera, symphony, and ballet in all of the capitals of the world.

The Metropolitan Opera of New York City has long been recognized as the richest and most talented operatic organization in the world. Never in musical history has there been an event with such fanfare and publicity as opening night at the new fifty million dollar Metropolitan Opera House at Lincoln Center in New York in September 1966.

The opera for the evening was the world premiere of Samuel Barber's *Antony and Cleopatra*. This new opera is based on Shakespeare's great drama. The ticket supply for the event was quickly exhausted, even though seats sold for as high as $250 for the evening's performance, and thousands were disappointed.

The part of Cleopatra in this fabulous premiere was one of the most coveted operatic roles of the decade. There was little speculation about the singer. For the first night at the new Met, Manager Rudolph Bing had made the obvious choice—the Metropolitan's greatest soprano of the decade, Leontyne Price of Laurel, Mississippi.

The fabled first night was a long way from her humble home in Laurel, Mississippi, but Leontyne Price was a girl who had risen against all odds, taking advantage of every opportunity, to gain recognition as one of the greatest singers of all time. Leontyne Price has not only proved herself a great singer; the quality of character she has displayed throughout her career marks her as one of the greatest American women.

Leontyne Price was born in Laurel in 1927. Raising children in the depression-filled 1930's was no easy task for her parents, James and Kate Price. Mr. Price worked in the local sawmills, but he often had to turn to odd jobs as a carpenter to maintain an income, and Mrs. Price had to help support the family with work as a midwife. Mrs. Price was a talented singer herself, a member of her church choir, and from the first knowledge that Leontyne had musical talent, Mr. and Mrs. Price persisted, making every sacrifice essential to getting the best schooling and musical training available to a Negro girl in Laurel. Leontyne began piano lessons with Mrs. Hattie McInnis at the age of three and a half, and from that time on she was involved in music at home, at school, and at church.

One of Miss Price's aunts was Mrs. Everlina Greer, who worked for a white couple, Mr. and Mrs. Alexander Chisholm, who expressed an early interest in the talented niece of their maid. Mr. Chisholm was a prominent Laurel banker. He and Mrs. Chisholm were more than willing to help contribute some of the cost of special training that special talent must receive if it is to develop its great artistic potential.

At Oak Park High School in Laurel Miss Price was always one of the student leaders, remembered as a particularly active cheer leader as well as a singer for most school ceremonial occasions. In the Negro community of the town she was always in demand for participation in church programs and for weddings and funerals. In her own mind was the question of how could she move from the center stage at Laurel to the world outside?

The start came when an Army chaplain at nearby Camp Shelby helped arrange a partial scholarship at Central State College in Wilberforce, Ohio. She registered for a public school music teacher's course, because that seemed the best professional opportunity, but by the time she had reached her senior year (through a combination of jobs, scholarships, and help from home) her plans had shifted toward the specialized training of the Juilliard School of Music in New York.

Miss Price's first recognition as a developing singing star came when Mr. and Mrs. Chisholm, together with the late A. Boyd Campbell and symphony conductor Ted Russell of Jackson, sponsored a special concert for her in Jackson in August of 1949. Her later stardom was no surprise to some of the hundreds who heard her in the Jackson concert, where she was accompanied by Mrs. Chisholm.

At the Juilliard School, Miss Price appeared in many of the school's concerts and operatic productions. There she attracted the attention of the composer Virgil Thompson, who asked her to take the leading role in a revival of his well-known modern opera *Four Saints in*

Three Acts. From this production she was signed for a starring role in a historic road company revival of the George Gershwin folk opera, *Porgy and Bess.* The *Porgy and Bess* production was a great theatrical as well as artistic success, throughout both the United States and Europe. At the height of this triumph Miss Price married William Warfield, the baritone who sang the role of Porgy.

In 1955 came significant new recognition. Miss Price was chosen to sing the title role in an NBC-TV production of the Verdi opera *Tosca.* The announcement of the forthcoming appearance of the first Negro in televised opera caused controversy and criticism all over the country, but most of it was forgotten when the performance, which was viewed by millions of people, demonstrated the soprano's mastery of the role.

Other significant operatic roles followed, on TV, with the great opera companies of Europe, and in concerts which showed her great affinity for modern composers. As her great talent developed she was put under contract by the Metropolitan Opera Company of New York, where she made her debut in 1961 in *Il Trovatore.*

The Met debut was typical of Miss Price's individuality, and her firm insistence upon recognition first of all as a performing artist. As part of her onstage operatic debut at San Francisco in 1957 she had appeared in *Aida,* and she repeated this triumph at Vienna in 1958, in the same style that would later make a critic at La Scala in Milan say that "our great Verdi would have found her the ideal Aida."

But as the fifth Negro to appear in the Metropolitan,

Miss Price did not want her first role to be that of the Ethiopian princess in the Verdi classic. She insisted on starting in a role where skin pigmentation played no part in the selection of the artist. After her Met debut, the impresarios were the first to admit the soundness of her judgment.

Her other roles that season further proved it. After singing the role of Leonora in *Il Trovatore*, she was just as convincing as the noblewoman Donna Anna in Mozart's *Don Giovanni*. After appearing as an Oriental in Puccini's *Turandot*, she gave a uniquely appealing performance as the same composer's Madame Butterfly. She then gave what many experienced critics hailed as the greatest rendition ever of Aida.

This was made clear when the Met paid her the supreme tribute of asking her to open the 1961–62 season with a performance in the starring role of Puccini's *Girl of the Golden West*. She thus became the first Negro ever to open a season at the Met. Her operatic performances from that time have continued to be a succession of new triumphs.

The special quality of Miss Price's voice is the capacity to send her soprano flooding through the Lincoln Center auditorium without straining. There is the assurance that there is still power to spare. No singer today possesses a voice that is more secure throughout its considerable range—the G below middle C to the D above high C— and with it the feather-lightness of a much smaller voice.

Her voice is her greatest achievement, but critics are quick to point out that she is not merely a superb singer, she is a superb actress as well. Her regal carriage sets off a stately figure. Her performance reflects a serenity which comes only through an inner strength of strong character, with none of the bravado and arrogance that sometimes reflect insecurity. She is quick to say that when she was first onstage at San Francisco "I enjoyed a real cold petrification," and a keen sense of the ridiculous protects her from the overbearing projection of vanity which too often afflicts many performing artists. She reminds interviewers: "I never go on stage without saying a prayer."

For her operatic roles, Miss Price usually uses a makeup that lightens her skin but does not change its color. "Corrective make-up I'm for," she has said, "but I don't believe in putting white stuff on me. Corrective make-up makes my own skin look more attractive. Some people have better sides than others. Why shouldn't you try to make your jaw look like Garbo's? I can accentuate my cheekbones or keep my nose from blotting out my eyes."

She has appeared on most of the great musical stages of the world, but Leontyne Price will always rank as one of her greatest experiences her homecoming performance at Laurel in 1963, when she presented a concert at Oak Park High School for the benefit of her church, the St. Paul Methodist. More than 2,000 persons from at least ten states, but mostly from Mississippi, overflowed the school auditorium and cafeteria. Some had to be seated on the stage to keep from turning them aside.

The unsegregated audience, one of the first in Mississippi, gave a tremendous response to the program which included a full repertoire to show the great range of the Price voice. There were repeated encores and standing ovations. Miss Price announced a special song for her aunt, Mrs. Greer, and as a final encore she presented the Negro spiritual "Ride On, King Jesus." There were no dry eyes in the audience.

In addition to her parents and other members of her family, the Alexander Chisholms were also honored guests at the concert. Through the years Mrs. Chisholm had not only been her benefactor, but also her friend and first fan. Mrs. Chisholm has described her part in Miss Price's career:

"I feel that God has favored us more than most by allowing us to participate in Leontyne's career. Our reward has been the fun—the privilege—of helping her when she needed it. I think someone with a talent like hers is one of God's chosen creatures."

Through the years new honors pile up for Leontyne Price. She participated in the inauguration of President Lyndon Johnson, and has sung at other official functions as representative of supreme American lyric talent. When the curtain dropped for the last time at the historic old Metropolitan Opera House in April of 1966, it was appropriate that Leontyne Price, as *prima donna* of the company, should ring down the curtain at the farewell gala.

It was even more appropriate for Miss Price to be the star of opening night at the new Met, glittering and exciting social event in the history of New York City. Prominent in the distinguished audience were her parents, Mr. and Mrs. Price from Laurel, and her brother George, an Army lieutenant colonel, given special leave to be on hand.

Miss Price's costume of golden cloth and jewels was

designed to evoke the riches and opulence of Cleopatra's court. She was so heavily costumed, said *Time* magazine, that "it was a wonder she could sing at all, though sing she did, and her burnished voice never sounded better."

From time to time Leontyne Price has made it clear that she prefers to stress her achievements as an American singer rather than as an American Negro singer.

"I know what I'm about," she has said, "but if I can't convince anybody else what I'm about, then my time is better spent trying to sing better. I've given up too much to let people who don't understand detour me. I don't 'react' in any way except like a normal human being. It is incidental that I am pigmented. I am a relaxed American. I am living what I have to say and singing what I have to say. I'm not going out in front of any groups. I am what I am.

"As to my background, I think my mother and my father were Mr. King and Mrs. Queen. My mother's flamboyant vivacity and wonderful sense of excitement —that's what gets me out onto the stage. And my father's character and pacing about life—that is what sustains me. That's the background I'm proud of. If that's Negroid, that's part of what it's all about. I'm just as proud of it as anybody whose family came over on the Mayflower.

"I'm living proof, living proof, that in everyday life I can move as a person, as an individual, a personality. It goes beyond singing, although I'm sure the Omnipotent had a plan when He gave me my talent. I'm not excited about being in certain social or nonsocial situations. I don't stop to be self-conscious any more."

Leontyne Price is now at the peak of a career that will rank her as one of the great singers of American and perhaps world history. In spite of that, she remains a vital, realistic young woman who recognizes the necessity for continuing hard work, knows how to make the most of opportunities affording pleasure and diversion, and—more important than anything else, perhaps—holds fast to a keen appreciation and enjoyment of other human beings. Thus her work as an artist is continually enriched by an instinctive understanding of human experience, while her life as an individual remains simple enough to make it possible for her neighbors to think of her as a neighbor and not as a prima donna.

Senator Blanche K. Bruce

Senator Blanche K. Bruce—A Matthew Brady portrait from the Library of Congress collection.

Blanche Kelso Bruce

Blanche Kelso Bruce, United States Senator from Mississippi, was born into slavery, but rose to achieve the highest Federal office within the gift of the people of his adopted state. The first Negro to serve a full term in the Senate, his record in that "most exclusive club in the world" compares favorably with other Senators of the period. By any standard, Blanche K. Bruce deserves rank as one of the more distinguished Mississippians in the century and a half of Mississippi's statehood.

The future Senator was born on a farm near Farmville, Virginia, on March 1, 1841. He was one of eleven children born to his slave mother. He never knew a father, and assumed that he was the natural son of the plantation owner whose name he took. The circumstances of his childhood and his early duties as a slave bear out that assumption.

Branch (his original given name) was assigned as the body servant to the legitimate son and heir of the plantation owner. The private tutor engaged to teach the young master also taught the young slave, contrary to the state ban against educating slaves, which had come as one of the results of the insurrection led by Nat Turner. During the 1850's Bruce went with his master to Brunswick, Missouri, where he learned the printer's trade as a printer's devil, and as a consequence improved upon the sketchy education he had received in Virginia.

Missouri was a slave state, but it was bitterly divided between Unionists and Secessionists with the coming of the Civil War, and never seceded from the Union. When young Bruce's master joined the Confederate Army, Branch seceded from slavery, and ran off to Lawrence, Kansas, and freedom. To emphasize the change in status, he changed his first name from Branch to Blanche.

Blanche K. Bruce went back to Missouri a few months later, but not to the territory still in dispute between Confederates and Unionists. He went to the town of Hannibal, on the Mississippi River in the northeast corner of the state. Hannibal is best known now as the home of Samuel L. Clemens, the great American writer who used the pseudonym Mark Twain. It is the locale of Twain's stories about Tom Sawyer, Becky Thatcher, Huckleberry Finn and his Negro friend Jim.

Hannibal became the site of what was probably the first public school for Negroes anywhere in the United States, founded by young Bruce in the midst of the war. A few months of teaching school convinced Bruce that he needed more education than the haphazard one which he had so far gained. Leaving his school in other hands, he enrolled in Oberlin College in Ohio, famous already for its special interest in offering educational opportunity to Negroes.

After two years, however, the young student had to yield to financial reality and go back to work to earn his living. For approximately a year he worked on the river steamer Columbia, which operated out of St. Louis, with a regular run up the Missouri River to Council

Bluffs, Iowa. Life on the river was often colorful, but it offered little permanent prospects for an ambitious young Negro. The stories he heard from those moving up and down the river all pointed to the deep South as a new land of opportunity. There was land to be acquired cheaply as a result of the impoverishment from the Civil War, and the newly freed Negro citizens would welcome as leaders energetic and educated men of their own race.

In 1868, Bruce visited Mississippi at the invitation of Samuel Ireland, a prominent Negro leader he had met in St. Louis. In Mississippi, Ireland introduced him to James L. Alcorn, the ex-Confederate general and delta planter who was establishing a new role as Republican political leader. Alcorn joined in an invitation to Bruce to settle in Mississippi.

At the age of twenty seven, with seventy-five cents in his pocket, Blanche K. Bruce moved to Floreyville on the Mississippi River in Bolivar County. The town of Floreyville was named for H .T. Florey, the principal landowner in the vicinity and a local, radical Republican political leader. Floreyville had begun as little more than a steamboat landing, but it quickly began to acquire the look of a river town in the first economic revival after the war. The region was still a frontier country, developing as new farm land was cleared and made accessible by new means of transportation.

It was to Florey and other Republican leaders of the area that the new citizen, Blanche Bruce, turned for political alliance, he helped them secure passage of a bill as a member of the state legislature to make Floreyville the Bolivar County seat. To gain this honor they had to dis-

place the interior town of Beulah. It was purely a local
issue in which they had the support of ex-Confederate
states' rights Democrats.

Young Bruce quickly established himself as a capable
and able citizen among his Bolivar County neighbors,
both white and black. They put him to work in their
school system as superintendent, and helped him make
the first payment on a plantation that was on the market.

When Bruce went to Jackson for the convening of the
legislature, he made a good impression among the members of the State Senate, who elected him their Sergeant-
at-Arms. When Governor Adelbert Ames removed the
sheriff and tax collector of Bolivar County, Bruce was a
nature choice to succeed him. In 1872, at the age of
thirty-one, he was elected to that office with an overwhelming majority. In later years he recalled one episode
in the campaign:

"I admitted that I had been a slave, but it was a
misfortune for which I was not responsible. . . . As a
slave I had been compelled to perform menial offices,
but I had served my master honestly and faithfully. Now
. . . I had outgrown the degradation and ignorance of
slavery and was a free man and a good citizen; but the
difference between my adversary and myself was . . .
well defined. Had he been a slave and performed menial
office, probably he never would have risen superior to
his original condition, and would be performing menial
offices even now. This sally was so well received by my
opponents my competitor never invited me thereafter to
debate jointly."

During the same year, Bruce was elected as the Bolivar County member of the Board of Mississippi Levee

Commissioners, a very important post in a Mississippi Delta county.

Before he could qualify for the office of tax collector, he had to file a bond for $125,000, but this was no great problem for the popular young planter and politician. Some of his chief supporters were white planters who supported the radical Republican faction, and they quickly signed his bond.

Bruce was one of twelve Negro sheriffs in Mississippi at this time, but his record was probably the most outstanding of any sheriff within the state, white or black, during a period of tensions and constant provocations to disorder. Even the most outspoken leaders of the Democratic party praised his conduct of the office, and they cooperated in helping to avoid the racial strife which plagued so much of the rest of the state and nearly brought it to civil war in 1875. In later years Colonel F. A. Montgomery whose book, *Reminiscenses of a Mississippian in Peace and War,* is one of the chief sources of delta history, frankly praised the Negro sheriff for his leadership. Even at the height of the fashion of later years to besmirch Reconstruction leaders in the state, it was never customary to deride Senator Bruce in Bolivar County, where his record was too well known.

Sheriff Bruce built the first house in Floreyville after the town became the county seat. It was a fine structure for the day, it became a residence of prominent white citizens after Bruce gave up his residence in Mississippi. (In 1876, after the Democrats had regained control of the state government, they changed the name of the town from Floreyville to Rosedale.)

Bruce was a delegate to the 1872 Republican National

Convention which renominated Ulysses S. Grant for his second term as President. While on the trip, he visited Washington with James Hill, a Negro from Marshall County who was Mississippi's Secretary of State. Hill later told how they visited the Senate Chamber (while the Senate was not in session), and the desks which had been used by Mississippi Senators were pointed out to them. Hill indicated one of the desks and asked Bruce:

"How would you like to occupy that seat?"

"What do you mean?" Bruce replied.

"Occupy it as a Senator from the State of Mississippi," Hill answered.

"It is out of the question," rejoined Bruce.

"I can and will put you there; no one can defeat you," Hill declared.

That was the beginning of a determined, low-key campaign which achieved victory in 1874. Along the way Bruce turned down a request from Governor Alcorn to run for Lieutenant Governor on his ticket, aware that the more important office would be open. Hirim G. Revels had been appointed to the Senate from Mississippi and became the first Negro Senator in American history, but his service was recognized as a stopgap from the first. Bruce sought the honor of a full term, won in his own right.

Senators were chosen by state legislatures prior to the adoption of the 17th Amendment to the Constitution, so Bruce's campaign had to be among the people who would make up the Mississippi state legislature in 1874. He carefully cultivated as many as possible with personal contacts, and his sponsor, Secretary Hill, kept him in close touch with all developments. The Floreyville *Star* led an editorial campaign in behalf of the election of a Negro Senator, with Bruce as the paper's pointed choice. Bruce's record as sheriff and his ability to work with all people were cited among his qualifications.

When the Mississippi legislature met in January 1874, it had a nominal Republican majority, but this was no assurance that it would elect a Negro Republican to the United States Senate. Many white members were opposed to the idea of choosing a Negro, and the result was the formation of separate white and Negro caucuses to consider candidates. Some whites adopted the strategy of nominating several Negroes in order to split up the votes of Negro members of the legislature. The Negro caucus refused to be divided by this stratagem and remained committed to Bruce.

The Bolivar sheriff was not without white friends, however. Thirty-six members of the legislature held notes due from the State Auditor of Public Accounts for back pay. Warrants had been given because the state lacked sufficient cash to meet its obligations, and the going value of the notes was sixty-five cents on the dollar. Under the law, however, a county sheriff could turn in the warrants at face value in transmitting county taxes due in payments to the state. Sheriff Bruce redeemed state warrants of legislators at face value and made valuable friends. When he was formally elected to the Senate on February 3, 1874, three white Democratic Senators were among those who voted for Bruce.

The new Congress met on March 5, 1875. Former President Andrew Johnson, now elected back to his old

Senate seat from Tennessee, was one of the new members, but the new Senator from Mississippi was the object of just as much attention. There was a dramatic incident at his oath-taking on opening day, which Bruce later described:

"When I came up to the Senate I knew no one except Senator Alcorn who was my colleague. When the names of the new Senators were called out for them to go up and take the oath, all the others except myself were escorted by their colleagues. Mr. Alcorn made no motion to escort me, but was buried behind a newspaper, and I concluded that I would go it alone. I had got about half-way up the aisle when a tall gentleman stepped up and said:

'Excuse me, Mr. Bruce, I did not until this moment see that you were without an escort. Permit me. My name is Conkling,' and he linked his arm in mine and we marched up to the desk together. I took the oath and then he escorted me back to my seat. Later in the day, when they were fixing up the committees, he asked if anyone was looking after my interests, and upon my informing him that there was not, and that I was myself most ignorant of my rights in the matter, he volunteered to attend to it, and as a result I was placed on some very good committees, and shortly afterwards got a chairmanship. I have always felt kindly toward Mr. Conkling since, and always shall."

Roscoe Conkling was the Republican Senator from New York, considered the greatest orator of his day. Conkling was for many years the leader of the conservative Republicans, both in the Senate and in national politics.

Conkling's courtesy to the new Senator resulted in a firm friendship. Bruce could usually be counted on to support the Republican leader on crucial issues, and his only son was named Roscoe Conkling Bruce. Alcorn's refusal to acknowledge his Mississippi colleague, even though they were both Republicans and Delta planters, was apparently part of a new personal political strategy for the former Governor, or perhaps it was lingering bitterness from the Governor's campaign in which Bruce had opposed him and supported Ames. Alcorn was disavowing all the radical Republicans in the hope of gaining new supporters among white voters in the state, and thus retaining his Senate seat. The effort was not successful, for Alcorn lost Negro support and made few converts among the whites. His successor, the Democrat L. Q. C. Lamar, was to be a far more cooperative colleague for Senator Bruce.

A tabulation of roll calls during the six years that Bruce served in the Senate shows that he ranked as a regular Republican, voting with the majority of the members of his party (which was the majority party in the Senate) approximately two-thirds of the time. The issues on which he differed show the quality of his statesmanship perhaps more than any other measure.

When a bill to exclude Chinese from immigrating to this country was in the process of passing by a large majority, Bruce spoke out briefly but strongly against it. President Hayes vetoed the bill, and its proponents could not muster the votes necessary to override the veto.

Bruce consistently proposed and spoke for measures for federal assistance in flood control on the Mississippi.

Alcorn had been making the same pleas without success, but Bruce is entitled to a fair part of the credit for the creation of the Mississippi River Commission in 1879. The establishment of this agency was the first major step toward the present flood control program which has eliminated much of the flood threat on the Mississippi River. The former member of the Mississippi Levee Commission did not forget the Delta's great need for flood protection.

During the last twenty-five years of the nineteenth century, the major economic issue before Congress was the effort to increase the money supply by providing for the free coinage of silver, or otherwise minting silver coins in larger proportion. Bruce believed that increased silver coinage would alleviate some of the debt problems of Mississippi farmers, stricken by the panic of 1873 while still in the grip of war born poverty. Consequently, Senator Bruce did not need the memorial from the Mississippi legislature to vote for the Bland Silver Bill in 1878. He voted for it out of conviction. His new colleague, Senator Lamar, voted against the bill because it violated his own convictions about government finance. As a result, the legislature, now controlled by the Democrats who had elected Lamar, passed a resolution commending Bruce and in effect censuring the new Senator.

Even though it was the state legislature which determined whether he would have another term in the Senate, Bruce was not politically naive enough to believe that the resolution of the Jackson solons offered any hope for his political future. The "Revolution of 1875" had thoroughly defeated the Republicans in Mississippi. Governor

Ames was forced to resign from office, and the extra-legal methods used to suppress or disallow Negro votes were now given official sanction. Negro participation in Mississippi politics had been sharply curtailed, and it was on the road toward virtual elimination. Senator Bruce consequently served the last five of his six years in the Senate with the knowledge that he could not be re-elected and that the day of another Negro Senator was in the distant future.

As a leading national Negro leader, however, he constantly spoke up in defense of his race, and against the betrayal of the southern Negro by his former allies. He blamed President Grant for the defeat of the Republicans in Mississippi, because he failed to provide troops to protect Negro voters. He also assailed the President for failure to support the seating of P. B. S. Pinchback as Senator from Louisiana. (Pinchback was a Negro political leader in that state, certified as elected, but never seated in the Senate.)

Bruce protested to no avail the irregularities in the 1875 election in Mississippi. Some of his comments in this connection have considerable relevance nearly a century later:

"Mr. President, do not misunderstand me; I do not hold that all the white people of the State of Mississippi aided and abetted the white-league organizations. There is in Mississippi a large and respectable element among the opposition who are not only honest in their recognition of the political rights of the colored citizen and deprecates the fraud and violence through which these rights have been assailed, but who would be glad to see the color line in politics abandoned and good-will obtain and govern among all classes of her people. But the fact is to be regretted that this better class of citizens in many parts of the state is dominated by a turbulent element of the opposition, known as the White League—a ferocious minority—and has thus far proved powerless to prevent the recurrence of the outrages it deprecates and deplores.

". . . . They [the Negroes] deprecate the establishment of the color line by the opposition, not only because the act is unwise and wrong in principle, but because it isolates them from the white men of the South, and forces them, in sheer self-protection and against their inclination, to act seemingly upon the basis of a race prejudice that they neither respect nor entertain. . . .

"It has been suggested as the popular sentiment of the country, that the colored citizen must no longer expect special legislation for their benefit, no exceptional interference by the National Government for their protection. If this is true . . . (it ignores the sentiment) that lies deep in the breasts of the patriotic millions of the country that the law must be enforced, and life, liberty, and property, alike to all and for all, be protected. . . ."

Throughout his term Bruce spoke out against legislation which provided for discrimination against the Negro. Sometimes his was the only voice raised, but his mere presence helped to hold back action which violated the spirit of the Fourteenth Amendment.

When the issue of the seating of Lamar came before the Senate following his election to succeed Alcorn, Bruce broke, as he had on occasion before, with the

Conkling Republicans, and voted to seat his fellow Mississippian. For four years Bruce and Lamar were cordial colleagues, working jointly on special Mississippi problems, and cooperating especially in regard to political appointments.

Each realized the differing political problems of the other, and, as Lamar expressed it in a letter to Bruce soliciting help about an appointment, "I do not wish to do anything that would bring you into a damaging conflict with your party friends."

The beginning of the term of President James A. Garfield coincided with the end of Bruce's service in the Senate. There was considerable talk of the Mississippi Senator's being named to Garfield's cabinet, and Lamar and four Mississippi Representatives (Chalmers, Money, Muldrow, and Singleton) let it be known that they supported Bruce for the appointment.

Garfield did offer Bruce the appointment of Minister to Brazil and then assistant Postmaster-General, but he rejected both positions. Eventually, he accepted the post of Registrar of the Treasury and was unanimously confirmed by the Senate after Lamar spoke in his behalf. As Registrar of the Treasury his signature appeared on all currency printed during his administration.

Bruce was only forty years old when his term in the Senate ended, and he continued an active life as one of the most prominent Negroes in America. In 1878 he had married Miss Josephine Wilson of Cleveland, Ohio, in the most impressive social event of the year for official Washington. They made a lavish honeymoon tour of the principal cities of Europe, entertained with formal receptions at the American embassies abroad, and they met leaders of government in France and England. Their residence in Washington became a meeting place for Negro political, business, and social leaders. In Washington, Bruce had become a firm friend of the prominent Negro leader Frederic Douglas, and the two had shared an apartment while Bruce was a bachelor. The circle of friends of Mrs. Bruce was not limited to Negro society, however; and wives of Supreme Court justices and cabinet officers were often entertained at her home.

When Democrats came to power in Washington in 1885, Bruce lost his post at the Treasury, but business and speaking engagements more than occupied his time. When President Harrison assumed office in 1889, he appointed Bruce as Recorder of Deeds for the District of Columbia. Bruce lost this post during Cleveland's second term, but was reappointed to it upon the election of President McKinley. He held this office when he died on May 17, 1898.

Blanche Kelso Bruce was a worthy recipient of high honors, of which he earned so many as the first of his race. Colonel Montgomery, his ex-Confederate political opponent and Bolivar County neighbor, remembered him as having "almost the manners of a Chesterfield."

Other former opponents in Mississippi remembered him as "always the gentleman, graceful, polished, self-assured, and never humble." But perhaps Bruce himself might have appreciated most the epitaph of the Raymond, Mississippi, *Gazette*, which remembered that Senator Bruce had often said, "I am a Negro, and proud of my race."

Senator L. Q. C. Lamar

Senator L. Q. C. Lamar—A Matthew Brady portrait from the
Library of Congress collection.

Lucius Q. C. Lamar

Lucius Quintus Cincinnatus Lamar, United States Senator, member of the cabinet, and Supreme Court Justice, had an eventful career which typified Mississippi leadership during the period of crisis at the time of secession, and of the Civil War, and the period of Reconstruction and reconciliation which followed. From a secessionist firebrand in his early days of political leadership, he became the South's foremost leader among the moderates who favored reconciliation to the results of the war and rekindling of a spirit of national unity. As a spokesman for moderation, Lamar was often the target for bitter attacks from the radical white leaders in his home state, but the wisdom of his course has been proven by the events of history.

Like most Mississippi leaders of the nineteenth century, L. Q. C. Lamar was born in another state. His family, of remote French ancestry, was one well known in early Georgia, where he was born in Putnam County on September 17, 1825. Although many Lamars were prominent in Georgia, the outstanding member of the family before Justice Lamar was Mirabeau Buonaparte Lamar, second president of the Republic of Texas.

L. Q. C. Lamar attended Emory College, then located at Oxford, Georgia, where he secured a good background in the classics, and also met his future wife,

Virginia Longstreet, the daughter of the president of the college. Augustus Baldwyn Longstreet was one of the foremost educators of the pre-Civil War South. He is best known today as the author of the classic of regional literature, *Georgia Scenes*. Judge Longstreet left Georgia in 1849 to take over the presidency of the University of Mississippi. It was natural for his son-in-law to follow to practice law in Oxford, Mississippi. Lamar supplemented his young lawyer's income by serving as an instructor in mathematics at the University.

Perhaps life in the shadow of his active father-in-law or the idea that political opportunity was greater in the state of his birth led Lamar back to Georgia in 1852. Two years later he narrowly lost the nomination to Congress from the Macon district. By 1855, Judge Longstreet had left Mississippi to become president of the University of South Carolina. Lamar returned to Mississippi, bought a plantation on the Tallahatchie River between Holly Springs and Oxford, and began the practice of law at Holly Springs. Within two years, he had been elected to the Congress from the district, sponsored by Secretary of the Interior Jacob Thompson, the former Congressman from Oxford. The Whig candidate whom Lamar defeated was James L. Alcorn of Coahoma County.

In the House of Representatives, Lamar lost no time in gaining a reputation as one of the outspoken firebrands who raised the threat of Southern secession if the will of the South was frustrated by national policy or legislation. As part of his threat he was grimly realistic about the effect of the dissolution of the Union:

"Dissolution cannot take place quietly; the vast and

complicated machinery of this government cannot be divided without general tumult, and, it may be ruin. When the sun of the Union sets it will go down in blood."

Perhaps Lamar hoped to win his points with Northern Congressmen by the very severity of his prediction. He was not guilty, like many Southern leaders, of minimizing the risk of secession. When the state congressional delegation caucused on the idea of secession in 1860, Lamar and Senator Jefferson Davis voted against it. They were more opposed to the timing than the idea itself, however. When the secession convention met at Jackson on January 7, 1861, Congressman Lamar was chairman of the committee named to prepare the ordinance of secession, which he drafted.

Although military life never appealed to him, Lamar accepted the personal consequences of the decision for secession and volunteered in the first Mississippi regiment which offered for service under the Confederate government. He was elected a lieutenant colonel in the regiment (the 19th Mississippi), which was commanded by his former law partner, Christopher Mott. When Mott, serving under General Joseph C. Johnston, was killed during the successful resistance to the invasion of the Virginia peninsula by the Union Army of General George C. McLellan, Lamar took over temporary command of his regiment. In this action it sustained twenty per cent casualties.

The rigors of military life in the field brought on an apoplectic attack which made Colonel Lamar a virtual invalid for months. In this limited-duty condition, he was a natural choice for President Davis to name as Confederate minister to Russia and special envoy to France and Great Britain. He was a man well qualified to make a good impression for the Confederacy on European leaders. His arrival was unfortunately almost coincidental with the disastrous Southern defeats at Gettysburg and Vicksburg which destroyed all hope of diplomatic success.

The former Congressman, soldier and diplomat returned to his farm in Mississippi at the end of the war. There was little chance for a successful practice of law at the time, but he welcomed an invitation to return to the faculty at the University, as professor of psychology, logic, and law.

Before many years, he was able to reenter politics. In 1872 Professor Lamar was returned to the House of Representatives as the first Democrat elected from Mississippi after the war. In Washington, he became the most prominent ex-Confederate in the Congress, not only as a veteran of the South's parliamentary battles before the war, but because of his ability as a debater and leader. Lamar pursued a deliberate course of conciliation, opposing the Reconstruction measures still being presented to the Congress but no longer denouncing Northern leaders. He waited for the most logical time to present his point of view to the nation as a whole. He knew it would be unpopular with the unregenerate fire-eaters at home who still spent most of their time bewailing the defeat of the Confederacy with little thought given to making a place for Mississippi in a united nation. Congressman Lamar regarded this as a duty more important than temporary popularity at home, and he did not hesitate to speak out when the chance came to him.

Senator Charles Sumner of Massachusetts was perhaps the most universally hated man in the South. Next to Thaddeus Stevens of Pennsylvania, he was the most prominent leader of the radical Republican reconstructionists in the Congress. Sumner's unpopularity in the South went back to the years before the war when he had been the Congressional leader of the abolitionists. He was far better known and hated in the South than Stevens.

When Sumner died in 1874, a day was set aside in the Congress for eulogies for the New Englander. The House was tense with anticipation when it learned that Lamar of Mississippi had asked for an opportunity to eulogize Sumner. Although well known in Washington, his quiet unassuming manner and sad grey eyes were unusual in this flamboyant period. As Lamar moved into extemporaneous oratory, however, those who heard him for the first time began to understand his magnetism. Lamar praised Sumner's character and ability, and then firmly made his points.

"Southerners, he said, cannot but cherish the recollections of the sacrifices endured, the battles fought, and the victories won in defense of their hapless cause. And respecting, as all true and brave men must respect, the martial spirit with which the men of the North vindicated the integrity of the Union, and their devotion to the principles of human freedom, they do not ask, they do not wish the North to strike the mementoes of her heroism and victory from either records or monuments or battle flags. They would rather that both sections would gather up the glories won by each section: not envious, but proud of each other, and regard them a common heritage of American valor.

"Let us hope that future generations, when they remember the deeds of heroism and devotion done on both sides, will speak not of Northern prowess and Southern courage, but of the heroism, fortitude, and courage of Americans in a war of ideas; a war in which each section signalized its consecration to the principles, as each understood them, of American liberty and of the Constitution received from their fathers. . . .

"Charles Sumner, in life, believed that all occasion for strife and distrust between the North and South had passed away, and that there no longer remained any cause for continued estrangement between these two sections of our common country. Are there not many of us who believe the same thing: Is not that the common sentiment—or if it is not, ought it not to be—of the great mass of our people, North and South? Bound to each other by a common Constitution, destined to live together under a common government, forming unitedly but a single member of the great family of nations, shall we not now at last endeavor to grow toward each other once more in heart, as we are already indissolubly linked to each other in fortunes? Shall we not . . . lay aside the concealments which serve only to perpetuate misunderstandings and distrust, and frankly confess that on both sides we most earnestly desire to be one; one not merely in community of language and literature and traditions and country; but more, and better than all that, one also in feeling and heart? . . .

"The South, prostrated, exhausted, drained of her life blood, as well as of her material resources, yet still honorable and true, accepts the bitter award of the bloody arbitrament without reservation, resolutely determined to abide the result with chivalrous fidelity; yet, as if struck dumb by the magnitude of her reverses, she suffers in silence. The North exultant in her triumph, and elated by success, still cherishes, as we are assured, a heart full of magnanimous emotions toward her disarmed and discomfited antagonist; and yet, as if mastered by some mysterious spell, silencing her better impulses, her words and acts are the words and acts of suspicion and distrust. Would that the spirit of the illustrious dead whom we lament today could speak from the grave to both parties to this deplorable discord in tones which would reach each and every heart throughout this broad territory: 'My countrymen, know one another and you will love one another.'"

The great Republican orator James G. Blaine was seen to turn away to hide his tears as Lamar finished. "My God, what a speech!" cried another Republican. "It will ring through the country."

It did ring through the country with lavish editorial praise which soon made it clear that the Mississippian was the nation's most highly regarded southern Democrat. In Mississippi, however, the reception of the speech was a different story. It was incomprehensible to many of his best friends that a white Mississippian could praise the man who had died with the admonition "Take care of the Civil Rights bill" on his lips. The Canton *Mail*, the Meridian *Mercury*, and the Columbus *Democrat* led an angry swarm of Mississippi newspapers which savagely attacked Lamar for making the speech praising the abolitionist. Many of those who had optimistically predicted new political successes for Lamar were quick to make known their disassociation. Some friends assured him that they agreed with both his sentiments and his tactics, but they were careful to express their views in the privacy of personal letters.

Despite this first reaction, the antagonism soon wore down. When the Democrats returned to power over the state in 1875, Lamar was the obvious choice to succeed Alcorn in the Senate. He was elected with a reputation already made as a Southern leader. Mississippians were still to express their anger and bitterness at him on occasion, but in the main they were to bask with pleasure in the reflected glory he brought their state for the rest of his life. L. Q. C. Lamar was never to be the popular, gregarious political hero, but a symbol of statesmanship for people who liked to think of a leader who is not one of the crowd.

Another sharp clash with predominant public opinion in Mississippi came early in Lamar's Senate career. The Bland Silver Bill was envisioned as a panacea by many farmers fighting debt and bankruptcy and many small town merchants feeling the same pincers which grasped Southern agriculture. The Mississippi legislature which had elected Lamar to the Senate petitioned and then instructed him to vote for the bill, but the former law teacher opposed it because of his innate economic conservatism.

In the closing hours of the debate on final passage of the Silver Bill, Lamar took the floor and asked the clerk to read the instructions which he had received from Mississippi. He then began his brief remarks, speaking extemporaneously, as always:

"Mr. President: Between these resolutions and my convictions there is a great gulf. . . . I cannot pass it. . . . Upon the youth of my state whom it has been my privilege to assist in education I have always endeavored to impress the belief that truth was better than falsehood, honesty better than policy, courage better than cowardice. Today my lessons confront me. Today I must be true or false, honest or cunning, faithful or unfaithful to my people. Even in this hour of their legislative displeasure and disprobation, I cannot vote as these resolutions direct.

"My reasons for my vote shall be given to my people. Then it will be for them to determine if adherence to my honest convictions has disqualified me from representing them; whether a difference of opinion upon a difficult and complicated subject to which I have given patient, long-continued, conscientious study, to which I have brought entire honesty and singleness of purpose, and upon which I have spent whatever ability God has given me, is now to separate us; . . . but be their present decision what it may, I know that the time is not far distant when they will recognize my action today as wise and just; and, armed with honest convictions of my duty, I shall calmly await the results, believing in the utterance of a great American that 'truth is omnipotent, and public justice certain.' "

Once again it was a speech which won wide praise over the North, but very little in Mississippi. *The Na-*

tion's comment pointed out both views: "for manliness, dignity and pathos (the speech) has never been surpassed in Congress. His vote will probably cost him his seat."

At home the attacks mounted. He wrote his wife:

"This world is a miserable one to me except in its connection with you. . . . I get a great many complimentary letters from the North, very few from Mississippi. . . . Can it be true that the South will condemn the disinterested love of those who, perceiving her real interests, offer their unarmored breasts as barriers against the invasion of error? . . . It is indeed a heavy cross to lay upon the heart of a public man to have to take a stand which causes the love and confidence of his constituents to flow away from him."

The hardest blow was not revealed until January 1879, when the *Clarion*, usually in the lead of those attacking Lamar, published a letter about his vote from his old friend, Jefferson Davis, who said:

"To deny the responsibility of the Representative to his constituency would be to attack the foundation of political system. If the people of a Congressional district were to assemble in mass and instruct their Representative upon any particular question, who will gainsay their right to do so, or his duty to obey? . . . It has been the practice of the Democracy either to obey instructions or to resign the office held from the people, so that their constituents might, if they so desired, select some one else who would more truly represent them. In opposition to the right of the constituency to instruct, I know of no argument which deserves notice, unless it be that which denies to the people the requisite amount of intelligence. . . ."

Lamar had never had to resort before to the traditional stump speaking campaign to win office, but he knew now that he had to fight back. He began a courthouse tour of the state, speaking to large audiences everywhere, and likening his role and vote on the Silver Bill to an incident in which he had participated in the Civil War.

Along with a large group of high ranking Confederate officers, he had been on a Confederate blockade runner approaching Savannah harbor. Before they entered the narrow waters of the harbor, the ship's captain instructed a young sailor named Billy Summers to climb the mast and see whether any Union ships were ahead. Billy reported that he saw enemy ships ahead. The distinguished officers among the passengers told the Captain that Billy was wrong. They knew from military intelligence reports that the Yankee fleet was not at Savannah. The Captain refused to go ahead, however, saying that admirals were greater military experts than he and Billy, but that Billy Summers at the top of the mast was a better judge of the immediate situation. When the ship finally did get to Savannah, it developed that Billy was right, and if they had gone ahead would have been lost or captured.

"Thus it is, my countrymen," Lamar pointed out the analogy, "you have sent me to the topmost mast, and I tell you what I see. If you say I must come down, I will obey without a murmur, for you cannot make me lie to you; . . . I prize the confidence of the people of Mississippi, but I never made popularity the standard of my action."

The people saw the light, and a new legislature in 1882 re-elected Senator Lamar by a large majority.

In sharp contrast with his predecessor Alcorn, Lamar worked easily in the Senate with his colleague Blanche K. Bruce. Both while he was in the Senate and afterwards, Bruce interceded for him with Republican administrations in regard to Mississippi problems, and Lamar did the same for him during the Democratic administrations of Grover Cleveland.

In Washington Lamar was welcome in top social circles. He was known as the one prominent Southerner admitted to the confidence and esteem of the Washington intellectuals of the day. His closest friend outside of government was the historian Henry Adams, great-grandson and grandson of Presidents from Massachusetts, who had been clerk to his father, Charles Francis Adams, in the American Embassy in London while Lamar was there representing the Confederacy. Adams prized Lamar as a raconteur whose stories of the Southern frontier were illuminations of America, and always praised him unreservedly.

When Grover Cleveland was elected President in 1884, he wanted an outstanding Southern member in his cabinet to symbolize national reconciliation after the Civil War. Even though Lamar was strongly recommending General Edward Carey Walthall of Mississippi for this honor, it was Lamar himself who was the obvious choice. National figures outside the normal political spectrum, like Carl Schurz and Henry Adams, were recommending the Mississippian, and there was wide respect everywhere for his integrity and intellectual ability.

L. Q. C. Lamar became Cleveland's Secretary of Interior and a major source of strength for the new President. His administration of the Interior Department soon made him a source of controversy and an embarrassment for Cleveland, as is usually the case when a public administrator does his job without fear or favor. As the man responsible for some of the vast government land holdings in the western states, Lamar took the first serious look at the depredations of some of the western cattle barons, who ruled much of the public domain and Indian reservations with hired gunmen (some to be romanticized later into "cowboys"), and at the bribery of corrupt Indian agents. Realizing that while regulation and the elimination of corruption would correct some of the evils, they could not really protect the land for the American people who owned it, Lamar recommended repeal of the basic laws under which many of the depredations were taking place. He proposed the repeal of the Desert Land Acts, the Timber Culture laws, and other legislation which was being used as a vehicle to consolidate huge corporate holdings, instead of making the land available to homesteaders migrating from the east.

These recommendations came in support of his Public Lands Commissioner, former Congressman William Andrew Jackson Sparks, who was not afraid to speak out in favor of reforming the existing public lands structure, which he called a nest of "fraud, favoritism and fees." With the support of Lamar and Cleveland, Sparks suspended all new entries into the public domain and even talked of requiring the railroad companies to meet the terms of their land grants, or return their acreage to the United States. Sparks estimated that during Lamar's tenure as Secretary more than forty million acres fraudulently acquired were restored to the public domain. At the end of his term President Cleveland claimed the restoration of eighty million acres during the four years.

Like many reformers, Sparks was more concerned about correcting the evils of the existing land grant situation than in carefully following the letter of the laws which he believed were responsible for many of the abuses. As the legal perfectionist, Lamar was offended by the zealousness with which Sparks attacked some of the railroads which had received grants, when he felt that they had merely followed the letter of the law. In consequence, the Secretary joined many western Senators in proposing Sparks' removal, which came under the next Secretary.

Lamar left the cabinet after less than three years of service. He came to the cabinet without any real concept of the vast natural resources it was his responsibility to protect, but his rigid recognition of the duty to preserve the American land heritage was a major factor in preparing the way for the first conscious governmental conservation policy under Theodore Roosevelt a few years later.

President Cleveland nominated Secretary Lamar to the Supreme Court of the United States on December 7, 1887. There was a predictable flurry of opposition to the appointment of an ex-Confederate, but it was mostly for political effect in the election of 1888 (where it did help contribute to Cleveland's defeat). The general reaction was typified by the comment of a New York newspaper: "Mr. Lamar is a sound lawyer . . . a dreamer, but a dreamer over the practical concerns of life." Despite these sentiments, he was confirmed by the Senate only by a close vote of 32 to 28, to become the only Mississippian who has ever served on the Supreme Court of the United States.

Mr. Justice Lamar's work on the bench belied his critics. During the five years of his service in the Court, he wrote his full share of opinions, but few of them relate to legal issues which have remained active. In the case of Clement vs. Packer, his opinion in regard to land surveys and evidence of boundaries established new law in an always heavily litigated field. Among other lawyers, his occasional vigorous dissents attracted as much attention as majority opinions. Judges and lawyers repeatedly referred to the style in which Lamar wrote his opinions: "faultless grace of diction," "lucid review," "great force and beauty."

In December 1892, Justice and Mrs. Lamar started South to spend the winter on the Mississippi coast. His health had been failing for a year, and doctors had prescribed a prolonged rest. At Atlanta he suffered a severe heart attack, but recovered temporarily and went to the home of a relative at Macon, Georgia, where he died on January 23, 1893.

No Mississippian has ever held higher federal office, and none has been more widely renowned and respected in the nation as a whole. His best epitaph will always be his own words:

"The liberty of this country and its great interests will

never be secure if its public men become mere menials to do the biddings of their constituents instead of being representatives in the true sense of the word, looking to the lasting prosperity and future interests of the whole country."

Jake Gibbs

Jake Gibbs crosses the plate after hitting a home run for the Yankees.

Jake Gibbs

Jake Gibbs, is a Mississippi athletic great who has proven himself in two areas of sport. As a college senior in 1960 he was named All-American at both football and baseball. He was at the very crest of sports glory, acclaimed by seasoned observers as the greatest triple threat back in the history of Southern football. He is generally conceded to be the most capable all-around quarterback in the history of Ole Miss football.

Young Gibbs then had his choice between a professional career in either baseball or football. He chose baseball because he loved the game more. The New York Yankees paid him the largest bonus ever paid by the richest baseball club in the country, but this was only the beginning of the Jake Gibbs story. Signing a bonus contract and becoming a Yankee regular are two entirely different feats, a hard lesson Jake had to learn. The story of how he became the regular catcher of the Bronx Bombers is one of the less heralded, but most dramatic, stories of modern-day baseball, a credit to the grit and determination of a young man who has shown himself a real All-American for personal integrity and courage.

But any story of Jake Gibbs should begin with his great days of college football glory. For Jerry Dean Gibbs, before he became Jake, the story begins in the century-old rural community of Elliott, south of Grenada, where he was born on November 7, 1938. As a child, he became involved in every type of team ball game, and at Grenada High School he became a local phenomenon as captain of the football, basketball, and baseball teams.

His parents, Mr. and Mrs. Frank Gibbs, were proud of his sports prowess, but they never pushed their boys to take specialized training. An older brother never became involved in school sports. Mrs. Gibbs had been the star player for Duck Hill High School basketball team, a sport that often involves physical contact, but she had to close her eyes and ask how the play came out when she saw her son headed into a bruising tackle.

In the hard brand of football coached at Ole Miss by Johnny Vaught, Gibbs did not become a regular until his junior year. He received some All-American mention that year, and in 1960 he led Ole Miss to its only undefeated season, and his unanimous choice as All-American. The highlight of that season was the final regular game, against Mississippi State. In the first half Gibbs completed nine straight passes, and was taken out for the second half, with Ole Miss safely ahead and others anxious to play.

Then somebody in the press box looked in the record book and noticed that the Southeastern Conference record was 12 straight completions, by Spence of Auburn playing against little Wofford in 1952. The word got down to Coach Vaught. With one minute and nine seconds left, Gibbs was sent back in. Ole Miss had the ball on its own 36.

Gibbs tossed 12 yards to Bobby Crespino (now with the New York Giants). He threw again, right into the arms of Art Doty. As he grabbed the ball, Doty was hit with a jarring tackle by State's Bobby Stacey, and the ball trickled out of his grasp. The record was lost, but Gibbs continued racing the clock for a touchdown, passing to men near the out-of-bounds markers in real professional style. He alternated between Crespino and Ralph Smith (Cleveland Browns) and, with two seconds to go, lined the last one up for Crespino in the end zone. State's Stacey was just as intent on stopping that last ignominious touchdown. He leaped and stole the ball from Crespino, and the ball game was over.

Jake Gibbs didn't learn about the missed record until after the game. When somebody compiled the season statistics a little later, they discovered that if the whistle had blown two seconds earlier, the Gibbs passing completion mark would have been .611 instead of .606, beating the record set by Fran Tarkenton (New York Giants) at Georgia in 1959.

The plaudits Jake Gibbs won from teammates, opposing players and coaches, pro scouts and sports writers could be listed indefinitely. Two worth quoting came from Knoxville, where Tennessee's Coach Bowden Wyatt said, "I don't see how a college football player could be any better." Tom Siler, the veteran sports writer and sports historian, called Gibbs the best triple threat ever to play on Tennessee's Shields-Watkins Field.

"Go (back) as far as you like," Siler said. (You can't) "name one better . . . George Cafego? Dixie Howell? Charley Trippi? Frank Sinkwich? Hank Lauricella? John Majors? Babe Parilli? Don Zimmerman? Jimmy Hitchcock?

"Leaf through the bright pages of football history, Southern style, and tell me a better package—passer, runner, kicker, defensive agent—than Jeremiah Dean Gibbs."

As a unanimous All-American with this kind of plaudit, Gibbs could have commanded a pro football bonus even higher than the undisclosed record-setting amount paid by the Yankees, but love of baseball and the challenge of the great Yankee tradition tipped the scales in that direction. After he signed in 1961, the next six years were to challenge fully every bit of his love of baseball. He had to battle every inch of the way to become the full-fledged Yankee that he is today.

Jake Gibbs had been a third baseman at Ole Miss. It was at that position he played on the Richmond Yankee farm club in 1961 and 1962. Respectable batting averages of .270 and .284 gained him a brief look-in with the Yankees at the end of the '62 season. His prospects for being called up as a regular were still remote, so Gibbs and the Yankee officials decided that he would have a better chance if he switched to catching. It was no easy switch to even consider, but Gibbs liked the glimpse of the possible future.

Elston Howard, one of the all-time Yankee greats, was at the height of his career at the time, not long after he himself had ousted Yogi Berra as the top catcher for the World Champions. Howard was actually celebrating his best year, being voted the American League's most valuable player, when Gibbs took on the job of becoming his successor.

Learning how to catch in the big leagues was like

arms of Art Doty. As he grabbed the ball, Doty was hit with a jarring tackle by State's Bobby Stacey, and the ball trickled out of his grasp. The record was lost, but Gibbs continued racing the clock for a touchdown, passing to men near the out-of-bounds markers in real professional style. He alternated between Crespino and Ralph Smith (Cleveland Browns) and, with two seconds to go, lined the last one up for Crespino in the end zone. State's Stacey was just as intent on stopping that last ignominious touchdown. He leaped and stole the ball from Crespino, and the ball game was over.

Jake Gibbs didn't learn about the missed record until after the game. When somebody compiled the season statistics a little later, they discovered that if the whistle had blown two seconds earlier, the Gibbs passing completion mark would have been .611 instead of .606, beating the record set by Fran Tarkenton (New York Giants) at Georgia in 1959.

The plaudits Jake Gibbs won from teammates, opposing players and coaches, pro scouts and sports writers could be listed indefinitely. Two worth quoting came from Knoxville, where Tennessee's Coach Bowden Wyatt said, "I don't see how a college football player could be any better." Tom Siler, the veteran sports writer and sports historian, called Gibbs the best triple threat ever to play on Tennessee's Shields-Watkins Field.

"Go (back) as far as you like," Siler said. (You can't) "name one better . . . George Cafego? Dixie Howell? Charley Trippi? Frank Sinkwich? Hank Lauricella? John Majors? Babe Parilli? Don Zimmerman? Jimmy Hitchcock?

"Leaf through the bright pages of football history, Southern style, and tell me a better package—passer, runner, kicker, defensive agent—than Jeremiah Dean Gibbs."

As a unanimous All-American with this kind of plaudit, Gibbs could have commanded a pro football bonus even higher than the undisclosed record-setting amount paid by the Yankees, but love of baseball and the challenge of the great Yankee tradition tipped the scales in that direction. After he signed in 1961, the next six years were to challenge fully every bit of his love of baseball. He had to battle every inch of the way to become the full-fledged Yankee that he is today.

Jake Gibbs had been a third baseman at Ole Miss. It was at that position he played on the Richmond Yankee farm club in 1961 and 1962. Respectable batting averages of .270 and .284 gained him a brief look-in with the Yankees at the end of the '62 season. His prospects for being called up as a regular were still remote, so Gibbs and the Yankee officials decided that he would have a better chance if he switched to catching. It was no easy switch to even consider, but Gibbs liked the glimpse of the possible future.

Elston Howard, one of the all-time Yankee greats, was at the height of his career at the time, not long after he himself had ousted Yogi Berra as the top catcher for the World Champions. Howard was actually celebrating his best year, being voted the American League's most valuable player, when Gibbs took on the job of becoming his successor.

Learning how to catch in the big leagues was like

going back to school again. In addition to getting to know all the inside baseball that a competent receiver must use in guiding a complete corps of pitchers, a catcher must learn to live with the seemingly endless bruised and broken fingers and assorted other injuries, minor and major, that make up part of his daily life. Gibbs had his share at Richmond and at Toledo in 1965. In 1966 he stayed the full year in New York, and was the starting catcher in nearly a third of the Yankee games.

The first year of the Yankee fall from the top of the league was that same 1966, of course, but Gibb's appearance had nothing to do with it, except as evidence that the veteran Howard had passed his prime. Jake Gibbs hit .258, and got some hits at crucial moments.

In 1967 Gibbs moved up to equal billing with Howard, and had played about as much as the older star when the latter was traded to the pennant bound Red Sox late in the season. From now on, for the foreseeable years ahead, Jake Gibbs is the Yankee catcher, one of the fixtures in the plans for rebuilding another baseball kingdom.

"Jake has that competitive urge," says Manager Ralph Houk. "He simply knows how to rise to the occasion."

Gibbs still makes his home in Mississippi, where he helps out with the coaching at Ole Miss during his baseball offseason. His wife is the former Patricia Monteith of Oakland. They have two young sons, Michael and Jerry.

As long as the Yankees include players like Jake Gibbs, Mississippi folk are not likely to be surprised if the Bronx Bombers get back in the running.

George Scott

Photo by James H. Peppler

George Scott and his mother at the George Scott Day parade at Greenville, November 16, 1967.

George Scott

When the young Red Sox rookie from Mississippi blasted home runs right and left, and compiled a batting average that had him riding at the American League's top early in the season, the baseball wiseacres were not impressed. It was merely the case of another spring sensation, they said, even if George Scott was elected the league's 1966 All-Star Game first baseman by his fellow players in the league.

"I told you so" was a common comment on Scott's performance in the second half of the season, which did not live up to one of the most sensational starts any rookie ever had in the major leagues. The pitchers around the circuit had discovered that the Boston first baseman had trouble with a curve ball outside, or most any pitch on the far side of the plate. On that steady diet his batting average fell off to .245 for the season, and he set a new and inglorious Red Sox club record of 152 strikeouts for the year. George's record wasn't by any means all bad, however. Mixed in with those strikeouts were 27 home runs and 90 runs batted in, 10 more than Carl Yastrzemski. And nowhere in the league was there a better fielding first baseman than rookie George Scott.

After 1967, it is hard to find anyone who will admit saying "I told you so" about Scott in 1966. Red Sox officials and sports writers, from manager Dick Williams on down, have rated Scott's performance as a major factor in the achievements of the miracle Red Sox, when they advanced from ninth place in 1966 to pennant winners in 1967.

The "sophomore jinx," the drop in performance of so many young rookie stars, is a tradition among major league ball players. For some it is merely a matter of an individual who can't stand prosperity, but for most it is the hard reality of opposing managers, coaches and players learning their weaknesses and capitalizing on the knowledge. By hard work and self-discipline George Scott overcame the jinx, and these same characteristics are likely to keep him a top-ranked major league star for years to come.

The story of George Scott's baseball career begins at Coleman High School in Greenville. Back of that is the story of the encouragement he received from his mother, Mrs. Magnolia Straw, to stay in school and not take the easy path of a dropout. George was born March 23, 1944, at Greenville. He credits the sacrifices and the constant encouragement of his mother with keeping him at Coleman High during the time when most Negro youths dropped out.

His high school coach, Albert Foules, and school principal, G. P. Maddox, are next among those to whom Scott generously gives credit for the success of his career. His natural fielding skill made him first aspire to play shortstop. That position in his high school, however, was already held down by a pretty fair athlete named Willie Richardson (now the star pass receiver of the Baltimore Colts) so he turned to third base. He played football and basketball, too, but baseball was always his favorite. Boston Scout Ed Scott signed him (with an assist from former Red Sox star Milt Bolling) out of high school.

Merely signing the Red Sox contract did not put him in Fenway Park, however. There were long seasons in minor league play at Olean, New York; Wellsville, New York; and Winston-Salem, North Carolina, before a climactic year at Pittsfield, Massachusetts, in 1965. Playing third base, Scott won the triple crown for the Eastern League, leading in batting average, runs batted in, and home runs, and clinching the crowns only with a great day at bat in the final day of the season. With those credentials he was naturally chosen the league's most valuable player and marked for likely transition to the parent Red Sox in 1966.

The Red Sox started him as their first baseman, and his performance with the bat put him in the All-Star game in July. After his poor performance in the second half of that season, Scott worked hard to correct his weaknesses at the plate. Under the special tutelage of former Red Sox-great Bobby Doerr, he cut down on his swing, which made it easier to check up and resist bad pitches. His home run total went down, but his batting average and overall effectiveness went up, and in 1967 he finished third in batting in the American League with an average of .304. Like most of the players of the go-go Red Sox of 1967, he turned in a peak performance blended into a team effort that made their team's achievement an all-time baseball miracle.

Manager Dick Williams had strict rules about physical

fitness for his athletes, and established a personal weight limit for each player. For six foot, two inch George Scott it was 215 pounds. When he showed up weighing 221 at Anaheim, at the start of an important three-game series with the California Angels, Manager Williams took him out of the lineup. With Scott on the bench, the Red Sox lost, 1–0 and 2–1. Some of the Red Sox players said such close observance of the rules had gone far enough, for a timely hit or two would have won both games. Scott weighed in on the third day at 217.

"Siebern will play first base," Manager Williams said. "I said before and I say again that George must get his weight down. He is not going to be allowed to get away with things that other players do not get away with."

The Red Sox lost again, 3–2. On the flight back to Boston that night, the stewardess served him the regular dinner, but Scott ate only the steak. At one point he swabbed butter on a roll, but then put it down without taking a bite and handed the tray back to the young lady with a sad look on his face. For the next game, against the Tigers on Tuesday night, he weighed in at 213, and he was back in the lineup.

"Come on, Twiggy, hit one out of here!" a fan behind the home plate screen shouted when Scott came to bat for the first time that night. George Scott did just that. [In addition to the home run he started a sensational 3-6-3 double play which brought the crowd to its feet cheering, for it preserved a shutout for Dave Morehead.] After the game, Scott told newspapermen, "I should be playing even if I weigh 500 pounds."

On the next night Scott hit two home runs off Dennis

McLain, one of the better Tiger pitchers, and then pulled a sensational play on the field when he put out Dick McAuliffe, unassisted, on what looked like a perfect drag bunt.

"Maybe The Man (Manager Williams) was right," Scott allowed after the game. "I never felt better in my life than I do at this weight."

Scott more than earns his pay with his bat, but some of the best critics of the game call him the best fielding first baseman to come along in years. After only a few years in the majors, they rank him as a fielder with Gil Hodges of the Dodgers and the fabulous George Sisler of the St. Louis Browns of nearly fifty years ago. If he is lucky enough to escape serious injury, he has a good chance to rank as the greatest fielding first baseman of all time.

"The difference between a good defensive fielder and one who is just out there," says Scott, "is that you think about the play you're going to make. A lot of people just get in a situation and then try to do something.

"In the 1967 World Series Maris was at bat and Lou Brock was on third. If Maris hit the ball, Brock was going to score. Maris hit one straight at me, and what I did was race down the line to tag Maris coming up at me. He had to come up at me and all the time I was keeping Brock from scoring.

"Sports writers crowded around and said they hadn't seen that play made in 15 years. They asked me what I would have done if he had hit the ball to the side. I would have tagged up and thrown to the plate."

George Scott has always been popular with the fans, wherever he has played. They like his good nature, and the way he always plays as hard as he can. The fans at Pittsfield, where he was managed by Eddie Popowski, now a Red Sox coach, came over to Boston in 1966, and gave him a special night.

The Red Sox star also took a bride from Massachusetts, where he had played so much baseball. On January 21, 1968, he married Miss Malvira Nancy Pena of West Falmouth.

The fan recognition he is proudest of, however, came from his home town of Greenville on November 16, 1967, when all of Greenville celebrated George Scott Day. There was a parade through downtown Greenville, for which the Mayor and scores of civic leaders turned out, followed by a banquet at Coleman High School. Scott rode at the head of the parade beside his proud mother, and the chance to honor her was what made it such a great day for George Scott.